I0663178

Polikushka

A Story of Redemption, Poverty & Human Dignity

A Modern Translation

Adapted for the Contemporary Reader

Leo Tolstoy

Translated by Tim Zengerink

Table of Contents

Preface - Message to the Reader

What If You Could Help Rebuild the Greatest Library in Human History?

Thousands of years ago, the Library of Alexandria stood as the crown jewel of human achievement — a sanctuary where the collected wisdom of every known civilization was gathered, preserved, and shared freely.

And then, it was lost.

Through fire, conquest, and the slow erosion of time, humanity lost not just books — but ideas, dreams, discoveries, and stories that could have changed the world forever.

Today, the Library of Alexandria lives again — and you are invited to be a part of its restoration.

Our mission is simple yet profound:

To rebuild the greatest library the world has ever known, and to translate all timeless works into every language and dialect, so that no seeker of knowledge is ever left behind again.

By joining our movement to rebuild the modern Library of Alexandria, you become part of an unprecedented mission:

- **Unlimited Access to the Greatest Audiobooks & eBooks Ever Written:**

  Instantly explore thousands of legendary works—Plato, Shakespeare, Jane Austen, Leo Tolstoy, and countless more. All instantly available to read or listen, placing a complete literary universe at your fingertips.

- **Beautiful Paperback & Deluxe Editions at Printing Cost**

  Own any title as an elegant paperback, deluxe hardcover, or stunning collectible boxset—offered to you at true printing cost, delivered straight to your door. Build your personal Library of Alexandria, crafted for beauty, built for durability, and worthy of proud display.

- **Fresh Translations for Modern Readers—in Every Language & Dialect**

  Enjoy timeless masterpieces reimagined in clear, contemporary language—no more outdated phrases or obscure references. Alongside the original versions, we're tirelessly translating these classics into every language and dialect imaginable, ensuring accessibility and understanding across cultures and generations.

- **Join a Global Renaissance of Literature & Knowledge**

  You directly support expanding our library, publishing deluxe editions at true cost, translating works into all global languages, and bringing humanity's greatest stories to people everywhere. By joining today, you're not just preserving a legacy of masterpieces; you set in motion a powerful wave of literary accessibility.

Become a Torchbearer of Knowledge.

Join us for free now at **LibraryofAlexandria.com**

Together, we will ensure that the light of human wisdom never fades again.

With gratitude and a shared love of knowledge,

The Modern Library of Alexandria Team

Visit:

www.libraryofalexandria.com

Or scan the code below:

Introduction

Tolstoy's Portrait of the Fragile Soul: Dignity Amid Despair

Among Leo Tolstoy's shorter works, Polikushka: A Story of a Russian Man holds a unique place as a powerful, psychologically rich exploration of poverty, redemption, and the quiet tragedy of human frailty. First published in 1863, this novella blends Tolstoy's early literary realism with the emerging spiritual and moral concerns that would later come to dominate his writing. The story centers around Polikushka, a downtrodden and alcoholic serf entrusted with a simple but important task: retrieving a sum of money for his mistress from a neighboring town. In this small assignment, a spark of hope is kindled in a man long forgotten by others and nearly forgotten by himself. But the unfolding narrative is not one of triumph, but of heartbreak—and, ultimately, spiritual clarity.

Polikushka is a study in contrasts. On one level, it is the story of a petty servant whose life seems irredeemably wasted. On another, it is a meditation on dignity, responsibility, and the fragility of hope in a world where social structures and personal demons conspire against redemption. Tolstoy's portrayal of his protagonist is neither sentimental nor condescending. Polikushka is not a symbol or an object of pity; he is a fully human character, caught between weakness and aspiration. The brilliance of the story lies in its capacity to elevate the ordinary—to show that even the most marginalized life contains depths of feeling, moments of transformation, and the haunting possibility of grace.

Set against the backdrop of a decaying aristocratic estate, the novella also serves as a quiet but sharp indictment of serfdom and the moral failures of the Russian nobility. While the story unfolds with the simplicity of a fable, its emotional and philosophical resonance places it firmly within the great tradition of Russian moral literature. It is both a snapshot of rural life and a universal exploration of the human condition.

The Moral Weight of Responsibility: Tragedy as Transformation

At the heart of Polikushka lies a profound moral dilemma: how do we respond when dignity is offered to someone who has never known it? Tolstoy presents this question not in the abstract, but in the form of a simple task given to a man whose life has been marked by failure. When the lady of the estate entrusts Polikushka with the mission to collect a sum of money, it is an act of unexpected faith. For a brief moment, the weight of his past is lifted. He straightens his shoulders, walks with new purpose, and begins to imagine a better future. His self-worth, long buried under humiliation and dependency, begins to stir.

Yet this moment of possibility is also a moment of enormous risk. The burden of responsibility—especially for someone unused to being trusted—becomes psychologically overwhelming. Tolstoy masterfully captures Polikushka's internal struggle as he wrestles with doubt, anxiety, and the terrible pressure of his assignment. When the money is lost, it is not only a financial loss; it is the shattering of a fragile new identity. Polikushka's unraveling is not melodramatic, but achingly human. We do not witness a fall from grace, but the breaking of a man who was just beginning to believe he could stand.

In this way, Polikushka becomes more than a tale of misfortune. It is a meditation on the cost of moral awakening in a society that provides little support for those seeking to rise. Tolstoy shows us how cruelty can be unintentional, how kindness without understanding can wound, and how even well-meaning systems can crush the souls they intend to uplift. But he also suggests that suffering, while not redemptive in itself, can lead to spiritual insight. Polikushka's final moments are filled with anguish, but also with a clarity that eluded him in life. It is a subtle but profound commentary on the dignity that remains even in the face of defeat.

This modern translation preserves Tolstoy's spare, vivid prose while making the language accessible to today's readers. Every effort has been made to retain the psychological nuance and emotional honesty of the original text, without softening its realism or oversimplifying its moral complexity. The goal is to bring contemporary readers into the world Tolstoy depicts—not just as observers, but as participants in its ethical questions and emotional truths.

In conclusion, Polikushka is a small masterpiece that deserves to be read alongside Tolstoy's greatest works. It reminds us that human value is not measured by success, that moral growth is often born of pain, and that even the most forgotten among us carry the weight of great spiritual possibility. In a world still shaped by inequality and disconnection, this story speaks with quiet urgency: about the risks of hope, the cost of trust, and the enduring strength of the human soul.

Chapter I.

Polikey worked as a servant for a noblewoman, though his job was small and unimportant. He lived in a tiny, run-down house with his wife and children.

The house had been built by the noblewoman's late husband and was very simple. It had just one room, about ten yards square, with thick stone walls. In the middle stood a large Russian stove, which helped warm the space. Each corner of the room was sectioned off, with one small area near the door called ''Polikey's corner.'' Inside the cramped space were a bed with a quilt and pillows, a baby's cradle, and a three-legged table where the family ate and did their washing. Polikey also used the table to prepare his materials for his side job as an amateur vet. A calf, some hens, the family's clothes, and basic household items filled every available spot. It was so crowded that moving around was difficult, but the stove helped by serving as a sleeping area at night and a table during the day.

It was hard to imagine how so many people managed to live in such a small space.

Polikey's wife, Akulina, was always busy. She washed clothes, spun thread, wove fabric, bleached linen, cooked, baked, and somehow still found time to gossip and argue with the neighbors.

The noblewoman's household provided them with a monthly supply of food, which was enough for the entire family. There was even extra grain to feed the cow. They received firewood and animal feed for free and were given a small plot of land where they could grow vegetables. In addition to their cow and calf, they also had some chickens.

Polikey's main job was to care for two stallions in the noblewoman's stables. He also treated the horses and cattle when they were sick by using syringes, plasters, and other remedies he had invented. For this work, he was paid in food and a small amount of money—enough for his family to live comfortably, maybe even happily.

But despite this, their lives were overshadowed by a heavy burden.

When Polikey was young, he worked in a horse-breeding farm in a nearby village. His boss was a well-known horse thief, a man with a terrible reputation who was eventually sent to Siberia for his crimes. Under this man's influence, Polikey learned bad habits and was drawn into a life of wrongdoing. Even when he wanted to stop, he couldn't—his early training had shaped him too much. He had no parents to guide him since they had died when he was still a child. There was no one to steer him toward an honest life.

On top of that, Polikey had a weakness for alcohol. He also had a habit of taking things that didn't belong to him whenever he could do so without getting caught. Small items like collar straps, padlocks, and bolts— sometimes even more valuable things—often ended up in his possession. But he never kept them for himself. Instead, he sold them, usually in exchange for whiskey, though sometimes for money.

As his neighbors saw it, stealing was an easy way to make a living. It required no education and little effort. But there was always a risk. If he was caught, he could end up in prison for a long time. This constant fear made life stressful for Polikey and his family.

Polikey almost got himself into serious trouble early in life. He married young and was blessed with a happy family. His wife, the daughter of a shepherd, was strong, smart, and hardworking. They had many children, and each one seemed better than the last.

Even after marriage, Polikey continued stealing. One day, he was caught with stolen items, including a pair of leather reins that belonged to another peasant. The owner beat him badly and reported him to Polikey's mistress.

From that moment, people became suspicious of him. He was caught stealing two more times, and the villagers began to treat him with contempt. The court clerk even threatened to send him into the army, which peasants considered a terrible punishment. His noble mistress scolded him harshly, and his wife was heartbroken over his behavior. Things went from bad to worse.

Despite his flaws, Polikey was a good-natured man. But his love for alcohol had taken over his life, making it hard for him to control his actions. He tried to quit drinking, but it never lasted. Whenever he came home drunk, his wife would curse at him and sometimes even beat him in frustration. He would cry like a child and say, "I am so unlucky! What should I do? If I ever drink again, may my eyes burst!"

But no matter how many times he swore to stop, it wouldn't be long before he disappeared for days on a drinking spree.

"Where does he even get the money for this?" the neighbors would whisper to each other, shaking their heads.

One of his worst mistakes was stealing an old clock from his mistress's estate. The clock was in her private office. It was so old that it no longer worked and was only kept as a family heirloom. One day, Polikey was in the office alone and, for some reason, felt drawn to the clock. Without thinking, he grabbed it and took it to a nearby town, where he easily found someone willing to buy it.

Unfortunately for Polikey, the shopkeeper who bought the clock was related to one of the noblewoman's servants. When he visited his relative on a holiday, he casually mentioned the purchase. Word quickly got back to the noblewoman, and an investigation began. Soon, all the details of the theft came to light.

Polikey was summoned before his mistress. When she confronted him, he broke down and confessed everything. He fell to his knees, begging for forgiveness. The noblewoman, a kindhearted person, didn't punish him right away. Instead, she spoke to him about God, the importance of his soul, and the future he was ruining for himself. She reminded him of the pain he was causing his wife and children. Her words touched Polikey so deeply that he sobbed uncontrollably.

Finally, she said, "I will forgive you this time, but only if you promise never to steal again."

Still crying, Polikey swore, "I will never steal again for the rest of my life! If I do, may the earth swallow me whole, and may my body be burned with red-hot irons!"

He went home, threw himself onto the stove, and spent the whole day crying and repeating the promise he had made.

After that, Polikey was never caught stealing again. But his life didn't get easier. The villagers still saw him as a thief and never truly trusted him. Whenever the time came to pick new soldiers for the army, the peasants all agreed that Polikey should be the first to go.

The estate superintendent also wanted to get rid of him and went to the noblewoman to ask her permission. But she, remembering how deeply Polikey had repented, refused to send him away. Instead, she told the superintendent to find someone else.

Chapter II.

One evening, Polikey sat on his bed by the table, preparing medicine for the cattle. Suddenly, the door swung open, and Aksiutka, a young servant from the court, ran in, gasping for breath.

"My mistress has ordered you to come to the court right away, Polikey Illitch!" she blurted out.

She paused to catch her breath, then continued, "Egor Mikhailovitch, the superintendent, spoke to our lady about sending you to the army. Your name was mentioned along with a few others. My mistress sent me to tell you to come immediately!"

Without waiting for a reply, Aksiutka rushed out as quickly as she had come.

Akulina, Polikey's wife, stayed silent. She stood up, grabbed his old, tattered boots—ones a soldier had once given him—and handed them to him without meeting his eyes.

"Are you going to change your shirt, Illitch?" she finally asked.

"No," Polikey replied.

Akulina still didn't look at him as he put on his boots and got ready to leave. Maybe it was better that way. His face was pale, and his lips trembled. He slowly combed his hair and was about to step out without a word when Akulina stopped him. She straightened the ribbon on his shirt, adjusted his coat slightly, and placed his hat on his head.

Then, without speaking, he walked out the door.

Their neighbors, a joiner and his wife, lived in the house next door. A thin wall separated the two families, so they could hear everything happening on either side. Not long after Polikey left, the neighbor's wife spoke up.

"So, Polikey Illitch, your mistress has sent for you!" she said loudly, making sure Akulina could hear.

That morning, Akulina had quarreled with the woman over something small—one of Polikey's children had done something to upset her. Now, hearing that Polikey had been summoned, the neighbor took pleasure in his troubles, thinking it was a bad sign.

"Maybe she's sending you to town to buy things for her household," she continued mockingly. "I wouldn't have guessed she'd choose such a 'trustworthy' man like you for an important errand! But if she does send you, bring me back a quarter-pound of tea, will you, Polikey Illitch?"

Akulina sat there, trying not to cry as she listened to her neighbor's cruel words. But as the woman kept talking, anger built up inside her. She wanted to do something—anything—to make her stop.

Then her thoughts drifted to something even worse. She glanced at her sleeping children and imagined them as orphans. What if Polikey was taken away? What if she became a soldier's widow? The thought filled her with fear, and she buried her face in her hands as she sat down on the bed, where some of her children were fast asleep.

A small voice suddenly broke through her sorrow.

"Mamushka, you're squishing me!" her child whimpered, tugging at her nightdress.

Akulina lifted her head slightly but kept her hands covering her face. "Maybe it would be better if we all just died," she whispered. "It seems like I only brought you into this world to suffer."

Unable to hold back her emotions any longer, she burst into sobs.

Hearing her cry only made the joiner's wife more amused. She hadn't forgotten their argument from earlier, and now she laughed loudly, finding joy in Akulina's misery.

Chapter III.

About half an hour later, the youngest child began to cry, and Akulina got up to feed the baby. She had stopped crying by then, but after feeding the infant, she sat back down and buried her face in her hands again. Her pale face only made her look more beautiful. She stared at the flickering candle and started to wonder why she had gotten married and why the Czar needed so many soldiers.

Then she heard footsteps outside and knew her husband was coming home. Quickly, she wiped away her tears and stood up to let him pass into the center of the room.

Polikey walked in with a proud expression, tossed his hat onto the bed, and hurriedly took off his coat. But he didn't say a word.

Akulina couldn't hold back her curiosity. "Well? What did she want?" she asked.

"Ha!" Polikey scoffed. "Everyone says Polikushka is the worst man in the village. But when there's an important job, who do they pick? Polikushka, of course."

"What kind of job?" Akulina asked hesitantly.

Polikey didn't answer right away. Instead, he lit his pipe, puffed on it a few times, and even spit on the floor before finally speaking.

With an air of importance, he said, "She wants me to go to town and collect a large sum of money from a merchant."

"You? Collect money?" Akulina asked in disbelief.

Polikey just shook his head and smiled smugly. "Yes. She told me, 'You are a man with a bad reputation, someone people don't trust. But I believe in you, and I'd rather give this task to you than anyone else.'"

He spoke loudly, making sure the neighbors on the other side of the wall could hear.

Polikey continued, "She reminded me that I promised to change, and she said she'd be the first to show me trust. She told me to go to the biggest merchant in town, collect the money, and bring it back to her. I told her, 'Whatever you ask, I will do it. I am happy to follow your orders.'

"Then she warned me, 'Do you understand that your whole future depends on how well you complete this task?' I told her, 'Yes, I understand. I will do my best. People have accused me of all kinds of things, but I have never betrayed you.' I convinced her that I was truly sorry for my past mistakes. She softened and said, 'If you succeed, I will give you the most trusted position at the court.'"

Akulina's eyes widened. "How much money are you supposed to collect?"

"Fifteen hundred rubles," Polikey said casually.

Akulina shook her head and asked, "When do you leave?"

"She told me to go tomorrow," Polikey answered. "'Take any horse you like,' she said. 'Meet me at the office before you leave, and I will see you off.'"

Akulina crossed herself and whispered, "God will help you, Illitch." She grabbed his sleeve and, in a trembling voice, pleaded, "Illitch, for God's sake, promise me you won't drink vodka. Swear on the cross that you won't break your promise!"

Polikey smirked. "Do you really think I'd touch a drop of vodka when I have so much money to handle?"

Before lying down, he said, "Akulina, make sure I have a clean shirt for the morning."

That night, Polikey and his wife went to sleep feeling hopeful, imagining a brighter future ahead.

Chapter IV.

Before dawn, when the stars were still visible in the sky, a small wagon stood outside Polikey's house. It was the same one the superintendent used, and hitched to it was a big, dark-brown mare named Baraban. Despite the cold wind and steady rain, Polikey's eldest daughter, Aniutka, stood outside barefoot, gripping the reins nervously with one hand. With the other, she clutched both her green and yellow coat and her father's sheepskin coat to keep warm.

Inside the house, everything was chaotic. It was still too dark for much light to enter through the patched-up windows, which were stuffed with rags and paper to block out the cold. Akulina had paused her cooking to help get Polikey ready for his journey. Most of the children were still huddled in bed, covered only with their mother's shawl since she had taken away the thick coat they usually shared.

Polikey's clean shirt was ready, but his shoes were in bad shape, worrying Akulina. Without hesitation, she pulled off her own thick wool socks and gave them to him. Then, she quickly worked on patching up his shoes, doing her best to keep his feet dry.

Meanwhile, Polikey sat on the edge of the bed, swinging his feet and fussing over his sash, complaining that it looked like a dirty rope. His daughter, bundled in a sheepskin coat, was sent to a neighbor's house to borrow a hat.

The small house buzzed with visitors from the court, each bringing Polikey little requests to pick up items for them in town. One wanted needles, another tea, and someone else asked for tobacco. Even the joiner's wife, who had quarreled with Akulina the day before, arrived with a cup of tea, hoping to make peace.

The borrowed hat never came, so Akulina had to repair Polikey's old one, which was full of holes and took some time to patch up.

At last, Polikey was ready. He climbed into the wagon, made the sign of the cross, and set off. Just as he was leaving, his little son Mishka ran outside, begging for a ride. Then his daughter Mashka appeared, insisting she wouldn't even need a coat if she could just have a short ride, too.

Polikey stopped the horse, and Akulina helped both children into the wagon, along with two more from a neighbor's family who also wanted a ride. As she lifted them in, she gave Polikey one final reminder of the promise he had made—not to drink a drop of vodka during the trip.

Polikey drove the children as far as the blacksmith's shop, where he stopped to let them out. "Go home now," he told them. Then, adjusting his clothes, straightening his hat, and pulling his coat tightly around him, he urged the horse into a trot.

Mishka and Mashka, both barefoot, ran home so fast that a strange dog from another village, startled by their speed, tucked its tail between its legs and ran off yelping.

The wind was sharp and cold, but Polikey barely noticed. He was lost in his thoughts, feeling proud of himself. "So this is what has become of me," he thought. "The man they wanted to send to Siberia, the one they threatened to turn into a soldier, the man everyone looked down on, called lazy, and accused of stealing. And now? Now I am the one my mistress trusts to collect a large sum of money. I'm riding the same wagon the superintendent uses when he represents the court. I have the same harness, the same leather collar, the same reins—everything."

Feeling important, Polikey straightened his back, adjusted his hat, buttoned his coat more tightly, and gave the horse a little kick to speed up the journey.

"Just imagine," Polikey thought to himself, "I'll have three thousand half-rubles in my hands, tucked safely in my coat. If I wanted to, I could run away to Odessa instead of bringing the money to my mistress. But no, I won't do that. She trusted me, and I'll make sure she gets every single ruble."

When he reached the first tavern, the mare instinctively turned her head toward it, as if out of habit. Polikey had been given money to buy food and drink, but he didn't stop. Instead, he snapped the reins and forced the horse to move on. The same thing happened at the next tavern, which looked even more inviting, but he kept his resolve and rode past without a second glance.

By midday, Polikey reached the town and stopped in front of the merchant's house where court messengers usually stayed. He led the horse through the gate, unhitched her, and gave her food. Afterward, he went inside and had lunch with the merchant's workers. While eating, he spoke about the important mission he was on, exaggerating his importance to entertain them. When he finished, he delivered the letter from his mistress to the merchant.

The merchant, knowing Polikey's reputation, was hesitant to hand over such a large sum. With a doubtful expression, he asked if Polikey had truly been sent to collect so much money.

Polikey pretended to be offended but couldn't quite pull it off. Instead, he simply smiled.

After reading the letter twice to be sure, the merchant finally handed over the money. Polikey carefully placed it inside his coat for safekeeping.

On his way back, he passed by many shops but didn't stop at any. He ignored the clothing stores and, when he had safely walked past them all, he felt proud of himself. "I have enough money to buy anything I want," he thought, "but I won't."

Still, he had errands to run. He went to the market and bought everything he had been asked to get. However, he couldn't resist stopping to admire a beautiful sheepskin coat. Curious, he asked the price. The shopkeeper, seeing Polikey's worn-out clothes, smirked as if doubting he could afford it. But Polikey proudly tapped his chest and said, "I could buy your whole shop if I wanted to."

To prove his point, he asked the merchant to take his measurements. He tried on the coat, running his hands over the soft fur and blowing on it to check its quality. He liked it a lot, but after a deep sigh, he took it off.

"It's too expensive," he said. "But if you could sell it for fifteen rubles..."

The merchant cut him off, snatching the coat back and tossing it aside, annoyed.

Polikey left the market and returned to the merchant's house, feeling pleased with himself.

That evening, after supper, he went to check on the mare and make sure everything was ready for the night. When he came back inside, he climbed onto the warm stove to rest. While lying there, he took out the envelope containing the money and studied it closely. He couldn't read, so he asked someone to tell him what was written on it. The writing simply stated that the envelope contained fifteen hundred rubles.

The envelope was made of rough paper and sealed with dark brown wax, with one large seal in the center and four smaller ones in the corners. Polikey carefully ran his fingers over it, even slipping one inside to touch the crisp banknotes. He was almost giddy with excitement, feeling an odd kind of joy at holding so much money.

After examining it for a while, he tucked the envelope inside the lining of his old, battered hat and placed it under his head before falling asleep. But throughout the night, he kept waking up. Each time, he reached for his hat to check if the money was still there. Every time he found it safe, he smiled, proud of himself.

"The same Polikey that everyone calls a thief," he thought, "was trusted with a huge sum of money. And I will return with it just as safely as the superintendent himself would."

Chapter V.

Before sunrise the next morning, Polikey got up, harnessed the mare, and checked his hat one more time to make sure the money was still there. Satisfied, he set off on his journey home.

As he rode, he kept taking off his hat to check the envelope. At one point, he thought, "Maybe I should put it inside my coat instead." But that would mean untying his sash, and he didn't want to bother with that yet. He decided to keep the money in his hat until he reached the halfway point, where he would stop to rest and feed his horse.

"The lining isn't sewn very well," he thought. "The envelope could slip out. Maybe I shouldn't take my hat off again until I get home."

He reassured himself that the money was safe and began imagining how pleased his mistress would be. In his mind, he could already see himself receiving five rubles as a reward. Feeling proud, he checked his hat one last time, found the envelope where he had left it, and pulled his hat down tightly over his ears, smiling at his good fortune.

But Akulina had only patched the hat in some places, and from all the times Polikey had taken it off, new holes had appeared. In the dim morning light, he didn't notice the tears in the fabric. When he tried to push the envelope deeper under the lining, one of its corners poked through the worn plush material.

As the sun rose higher in the sky, the warmth made Polikey drowsy. Since he had barely slept the night before, he dozed off in the wagon, his head bobbing up and down as the horse trotted along. Each time his head jerked forward, the envelope slipped further through the hole in his hat.

He didn't wake up until he was nearly home. His first instinct was to pat his hat to make sure it was still on his head. Feeling it there, he didn't think to check inside for the money. Instead, he gave the mare a light tap with the whip, urging her forward, and started thinking about how much he would be rewarded.

Feeling confident, Polikey glanced around with the air of a man who had already secured a respected position at the court. As he neared the village, he saw his small house in the distance. His neighbor, the joiner's wife, was carrying rolls of linen. He could also see the court office and his mistress's home—the place where he would soon prove himself as a trustworthy and honest man.

"People can say all kinds of things about you," he thought, "but the truth always comes out. When my mistress sees me, she'll say, 'Well done, Polikey! You've proven yourself. Here's three—maybe five—perhaps even ten rubles for you!' She might even offer me tea or a little vodka—who knows?"

The thought of vodka warmed him up. He was cold from the journey, and the idea of celebrating made him even more excited.

"What a wonderful holiday we'll have if she gives me ten rubles!" he said aloud. "I could finally pay Nikita the four rubles and fifty kopecks I owe him and still have enough left to buy shoes for the children."

As he neared his house, Polikey straightened his coat, smoothed his fur collar, retied his sash, and ran a hand through his hair. To do that, he had to take off his hat. But as he did, he reached inside the lining for the envelope.

It wasn't there.

His fingers moved faster, searching every corner of the hat. His heart pounded. He used both hands, checking again and again, but the money was gone.

His face turned pale. With shaking hands, he ran his fingers through the crown of his tattered hat, hoping to find the envelope stuck somewhere inside. Nothing.

He stopped the mare and frantically searched the wagon, flipping over everything inside. When he found nothing, he patted down all his pockets. But the money was nowhere to be found.

Grabbing his head in despair, he cried out, "Oh God, what have I done? What will happen to me now?"

Then, realizing he was near his neighbors' house and that people could see him, he forced himself to stay calm. Pulling his hat down tightly, he turned the horse around and rode back the way he came, desperately hoping to find the missing money.

Chapter VI.

The whole day passed, and no one in the village of Pokrovski saw any sign of Polikey. His mistress kept asking where he was, and she sent Aksiutka several times to check with Akulina. Each time, Akulina said he hadn't come home yet. She guessed that maybe the merchant had kept him late or that something had happened to the horse.

Polikey's wife felt a deep worry in her heart. She could barely focus on her chores as she prepared for the next day, which was a holiday. Their children were also waiting anxiously for their father, though for different reasons. While the noblewoman and Akulina were only worried about Polikey's safety, the children were eager to see what gifts he might bring from town.

The only news about Polikey that day came from some nearby peasants. They said they saw him running along the road, asking people if they had found an envelope. One man also saw him walking beside his exhausted horse. "I thought he was drunk," the man said, "or maybe he hadn't fed the poor animal in days—it looked so weak."

That night, Akulina lay awake, unable to sleep. Every little sound made her heart race, hoping it was Polikey returning home. But he never came. When the rooster crowed for the third time, she had to get up to start the fire. The first light of morning was appearing, and the church bells had begun to ring. Soon, the children were awake too, but still, there was no sign of their father.

The morning was bitterly cold. When Akulina looked outside, she saw thick snow covering the houses, fields, and roads. The sky was clear, as if the cold weather was fitting for the holiday they were about to celebrate. From their home, they could see far down the road, but there was no one in sight.

Akulina was busy baking when suddenly, she heard the excited shouts of her children. A moment later, Polikey stepped inside, carrying a bundle in his hand. He walked straight to his corner without a word. Akulina noticed how pale he looked, his face full of sorrow, as if he wanted to cry but couldn't. But instead of questioning him right away, she asked quickly, "Illitch, is everything okay?"

Polikey muttered something, but she couldn't understand him.

"What?" she asked again. "Did you see our mistress?"

Polikey sat on the bed, staring blankly and forcing a bitter smile. He didn't answer right away. When Akulina asked again, he finally said, "Akulina, I gave the money to our mistress, and oh, how she thanked me!" Then, his expression changed. He suddenly looked around the room, his eyes full of worry. His gaze lingered on two things: the baby in the cradle and a rope hanging from the ladder.

Without saying anything, he walked over to the cradle and quickly began untying the knot in the rope. Once it was free, he stood still for a moment, silently looking at the baby.

Akulina, too busy with her baking, didn't notice. She placed her cakes in the corner, while Polikey quietly hid the rope under his coat and sat back down.

"What's wrong, Illitch?" she asked. "You don't seem yourself."

"I haven't slept," he replied.

Just then, a shadow passed by the window. Moments later, Aksiutka burst into the room.

"The mistress is calling for you, Polikey Illitch! She says you must come right away!"

Polikey looked at Akulina, then at the girl.

"Right away?" he repeated. "What more could she want?"

His voice was so soft that Akulina felt a little relieved, thinking maybe their mistress wanted to reward him.

"Tell her I'm coming," he said.

But instead of following the girl, Polikey went somewhere else.

At the front of the house, a ladder led up to the attic. He glanced around, making sure no one was watching. Then, he quickly climbed up.

Meanwhile, Aksiutka arrived at her mistress's house.

"Why hasn't Polikey come yet?" the noblewoman asked impatiently. "Where is he? Why is he taking so long?"

Aksiutka quickly ran back to his house and demanded to see him.

"He left a while ago," Akulina replied. She looked around nervously before adding, "Maybe he stopped somewhere and fell asleep on the way."

Around this time, the joiner's wife climbed up to the attic to collect some linen she had left to dry. Suddenly, a terrible scream filled the air. Moments later, she came rushing down the ladder, her hair a mess and her clothes wrinkled. Her face was pale with fear.

"Illitch—he hanged himself!" she cried.

Akulina, horrified, ran up the ladder before anyone could stop her. The sight that met her eyes made her let out a heart-wrenching scream before she fainted. She fell backward, and if not for a nearby villager who caught her in his arms, she might have been seriously hurt.

Later that same day, just before nightfall, a villager returning from town found the missing envelope with Polikey's money lying on the side of the road. He quickly brought it back to the noblewoman.

It was during the time of serfdom, long before Alexander II freed sixty million serfs in 1862. Back then, peasants were ruled by different kinds of landowners. Some were kind and treated their serfs well, remembering that they, too, were human. But others were cruel, showing no kindness at all. The worst of them were former serfs who had risen to power and now ruled over others.

These new officials, once peasants themselves, often treated their fellow peasants with even more harshness than noble-born masters. Many of them had been promoted to oversee large estates, and instead of leading fairly, they made life miserable for those under them.

Peasants had to work for their master a set number of days each week. The land was rich, and there was plenty of water, forests, and meadows to meet the needs of both the landowner and the workers. But when one nobleman appointed a former peasant as his new estate manager, things took a terrible turn.

As soon as this man, Michael Simeonovitch, was given authority, he began abusing his power. He forced the peasants to work more days than the law required. He even opened a brick factory and made men and women work long hours there, selling the bricks for his own profit.

At one point, the exhausted peasants decided to seek justice. They sent a small group to Moscow to complain directly to their master. But when they returned, they had no good news—nothing had changed. Their attempt to get help only made things worse. Michael was furious that they had gone above him, and he took revenge by making their lives even harder.

Some peasants, hoping to gain favor with Michael, betrayed their own people. They made up lies, accusing others of wrongdoing, which led to even more punishments. Fear spread through the village. Whenever Michael walked through, people would run and hide as if he were a wild animal. Seeing how much power he had over them, he became even more ruthless.

Forced to work endlessly and suffering constant mistreatment, the lives of the serfs became unbearable.

There was a time when peasants, pushed to their limits, could find ways to get rid of cruel overseers like Simeonovitch. These desperate people started wondering if there was any way to escape their unbearable suffering. They held secret meetings in hidden places, sharing their misery and discussing possible solutions. Sometimes, the boldest among them would stand up and say, "How much longer can we let this man control us? We should put an end to this now. It's better to die fighting than to live in endless suffering. Getting rid of such an evil man can't be wrong."

One day, just before Easter, a group of peasants gathered in the woods where Michael had sent them to clear land for their master. At lunchtime, they sat together to eat and talk.

"Why don't we just leave?" one of them asked. "Soon, we'll have nothing left. We're already worked to death—day and night, with no rest for us or our wives.

If we make the smallest mistake, he punishes us. Remember poor Simeon? He beat him to death. And Anisim? He was tortured in chains until he died. We can't take this anymore."

Another man added, "So why wait? Let's act now. Michael is coming this evening. He'll insult us and treat us like animals, just like always. Let's knock him off his horse and end this with a single strike of an axe. Then we'll bury him deep in the ground where no one will ever find him. But we all have to stick together and not betray each other."

The man who spoke last was Vasili Minayeff. He had more reason than anyone to hate Michael. The overseer whipped him every week and even took Vasili's wife to work as his personal cook.

That evening, just as they had expected, Michael arrived on horseback. Right away, he started shouting about how poorly the work had been done. Then he noticed that some lime trees had been cut down.

"I told you not to cut those trees!" he yelled angrily. "Who did this? Tell me now, or I'll have every one of you whipped!"

After checking, they pointed to a man named Sidor as the one responsible. Michael slapped him across the face and then turned to Vasili, punishing him too for not working hard enough. When he was satisfied, he rode away, unharmed.

That night, the peasants gathered again. Vasili, furious, spoke up.

"What kind of men are we?" he asked. "We're not men at all—we're just weak little sparrows! We swore we'd stand together, but the moment we had the chance, we ran and hid. It reminds me of a story: once, a group of sparrows decided to fight back against a hawk. But as soon as the hawk appeared, they all scattered into the grass. The hawk grabbed one of them and flew away. The other sparrows then came out, chirping sadly. 'Who got caught?' they asked. 'Vanka!' someone answered. 'Well, he probably deserved it.' That's exactly how you all acted today. When Michael attacked Sidor, why didn't we do what we agreed on? Why didn't we strike him down and free ourselves from this nightmare?"

His words filled the peasants with guilt and determination. They were now more convinced than ever that Michael had to die.

Not long after, Michael gave orders that they were to work even during the Easter holiday, plowing and planting oats. This news crushed the serfs. They gathered once again at Vasili's house, angry and desperate.

"If he has no fear of God and keeps treating us this way," someone said, "then we must end it. If not, we might as well be dead already."

But one man, Peter Mikhayeff, disagreed. He was a peaceful man and tried to calm them down.

"Brothers," he said, "you're thinking about doing something terrible. Taking a life is not something to take lightly. It's easy to kill a man, but what will happen to our souls if we do it? If Michael continues to be cruel, God will punish him in His own way. We just need to be patient."

But Vasili was furious.

"Peter always says the same thing—'It's a sin to kill.' Of course, it's wrong to kill a good man! But we're not talking about an innocent person here. Even God would strike down someone as cruel as Michael. Think about it—if a dog goes mad, we have to put it down. Otherwise, it will bite and hurt more people. Leaving him alive is the real sin. If we're going to suffer, let's at least do it for a cause. Others will thank us for ending his cruelty.

"And Peter, you're talking about sin? Isn't it also a sin to work during Easter? Yet, you won't be working, will you?"

Peter sighed and replied, "If they force me to plow, I will go. But it won't be by my own choice. God will know who is truly at fault, and He will punish the one responsible. But we must not forget what's right. I'm not just sharing my own opinion. God's law tells us not to fight evil with more evil. If we try to get rid of wickedness through violence, it will only come back stronger. Killing a man might seem easy, but his blood will stain your soul forever. You may think you've gotten rid of a cruel person, but in reality, you will only be planting the seeds of even greater wrongdoing. If you give in to hatred, it will consume you."

Some of the peasants agreed with Peter, while others supported Vasili. Soon, the group was divided into two sides—one that believed in fighting back and one that believed in patience.

On Easter Sunday, no work was done. That evening, an elder from the nobleman's court arrived with a message. "Michael Simeonovitch, the superintendent, has ordered you all to plow the fields for oats tomorrow." He went from house to house, assigning different groups of men to different parts of the land— some by the river, others near the road. The peasants were devastated. Many of them wept, but no one dared to refuse.

The next morning, while the church bells rang and the rest of the village prepared to celebrate, the exhausted serfs went to the fields instead. Meanwhile, Michael woke up late and strolled around the estate. His servants had already finished their chores and changed into clean clothes for the holiday. His wife and widowed daughter, who was visiting for Easter as usual, had returned from church. They sat down to drink tea, with a steaming samovar in front of them.

As Michael lit his pipe, he called for the elder.

"Well," he asked, "did you give the peasants their orders?"

"Yes, sir," the elder replied.

"Did they go to the fields?"

"Yes, sir. I personally told them where to start."

"Good. But just giving orders isn't enough. Are they actually plowing? Go check right now. Tell them I'll be there after lunch, and I expect to see one and a half acres plowed for every two plows. The work must be done properly, or they'll be punished—holiday or not."

"I understand, sir," the elder said, ready to leave.

But Michael stopped him. He hesitated for a moment, as if something was bothering him. Then he added, "Listen carefully to what those peasants are saying about me. I know how they think. They're lazy and always complaining. They'd rather lie around all day instead of working. They want to feast and celebrate, but they don't understand that if the fields aren't plowed in time, it'll be too late. Go listen to them and tell me exactly what they say about me."

"I understand, sir," the elder repeated before riding off to the fields.

Michael's wife, a kind-hearted woman, had overheard the conversation. She stepped closer and gently pleaded with him.

"My dear Mishinka," she said, using his nickname, "please think about the meaning of this holy day. Don't sin on such an important occasion. Let the poor peasants go home."

Michael chuckled but didn't answer right away. Finally, he smirked and said, "You haven't been punished in a long time, and now you think you can interfere in things that don't concern you."

"Mishinka," she insisted, "I had a terrible dream about you last night. Please, let them go."

He scoffed. "Oh, so now you've gotten fatter and think you wouldn't feel the whip?" he sneered. "Be careful."

Michael shoved his hot pipe against his wife's cheek and chased her out of the room. Then he sat down for a big meal. He ate cabbage soup, roast pork, meat pie, pastries with milk, jelly, sweet cakes, and drank vodka. After finishing, he called his cook over, told her to sit down, and ordered her to sing while he played the guitar.

As Michael enjoyed himself, the elder returned. He bowed low before speaking.

"Well," Michael asked, "did they plow?"

"Yes," the elder replied. "They've finished about half the field."

"Any problems?"

"No, sir. The work is well done. They're afraid of you."

"How's the soil?"

"Very soft, sir."

Michael paused before asking, "And what did they say about me? They must have cursed me, right?"

The elder hesitated, but Michael ordered him to speak. "Tell me exactly what they said. If you tell the truth, I'll reward you. If you hide anything, you'll be punished. Catherine, pour him a glass of vodka to loosen his tongue!"

The elder drank and thought to himself, "It's not my fault if they don't like him. I'll just tell the truth." Then he turned back to Michael and said, "They complained, sir. They complained a lot."

Michael smirked. "And what exactly did they say?"

"Well, they said you don't believe in God."

Michael laughed. "Who said that?"

"They all agreed on it. Some even said you've been taken over by evil."

Michael chuckled. "Interesting. What else? What did Vasili say?"

The elder didn't want to betray the peasants, but he had a personal grudge against Vasili. So he said, "Vasili cursed you more than anyone."

Michael's eyes narrowed. "What did he say?"

"It's terrible to repeat, sir. But he said, 'He will die like a dog, without a chance to repent.'"

Michael slammed his fist on the table. "That traitor! If he wasn't so afraid, he'd try to kill me himself. Fine, Vasili—we'll deal with you soon. And what about Tishka? Did he call me a dog?"

"Well," the elder admitted, "none of them spoke kindly of you. But honestly, I feel bad repeating their words."

"Whether you like it or not, I want to hear everything!" Michael snapped.

"Some said your back should be broken."

Michael threw his head back and laughed. "We'll see whose back breaks first," he sneered. "Was that Tishka's idea? I knew they wouldn't say nice things about me, but I didn't expect so many threats. And what about Peter Mikhayeff? That fool—was he cursing me too?"

"No, sir," the elder said. "Peter didn't curse you at all. He was the only one who stayed silent. He's a very wise man, and the other peasants were shocked by what he did."

"What did he do?"

"He did something strange. He was plowing, and as I got closer, I heard someone singing. Then I saw something glowing between his plowshares."

Michael sat up. "Well? What was it?"

"It was a small wax candle, burning brightly. Even with the wind, it didn't go out. Peter, wearing a clean new shirt, was singing hymns while he plowed. No matter how he moved, the candle kept burning. I watched as he shook the plow hard, but the little flame didn't even flicker."

Michael's grin faded. "And what did he say?"

"Not much. When he saw me, he simply greeted me for the holiday and went back to singing and plowing. The other peasants, however, mocked him. They laughed and said, 'It's a terrible sin to plow on Easter Monday. Even if you prayed for the rest of your life, you wouldn't be forgiven.'"

"And what did Peter say to that?"

"He stopped just long enough to say, 'There should be peace on earth and goodwill to men.' Then he kept working, and the candle burned even brighter."

Michael no longer found the conversation amusing. He set his guitar aside, his head dropping forward as he sank into deep thought.

Then, without another word, he ordered the elder and the cook to leave. Once alone, he slipped behind a screen and collapsed onto his bed, sighing and moaning as if something was weighing heavily on him.

His wife soon came in and spoke to him gently, trying to comfort him. But he shook his head and refused to listen.

"He has defeated me," Michael whispered, "and my end is near."

"Mishinka," his wife pleaded, "get up and go to the peasants in the field. Let them go home, and everything will be fine. You've faced much bigger risks before without fear, but now you seem truly afraid."

"He has defeated me," Michael muttered again. "I am finished."

His wife grew frustrated. "What are you talking about? If you just do as I say, there's nothing to worry about." Then, softening her tone, she added, "Come on, Mishinka. I'll have the horse saddled for you right away."

When the horse was ready, she convinced her husband to get on and ride to the fields to free the peasants. As Michael arrived in the village, a woman opened the gate for him. But as soon as people spotted him, fear spread through the streets. Everyone rushed to hide—ducking into houses, gardens, or any place they could avoid being seen.

When he reached the far gate, he found it closed. Since he couldn't open it while on horseback, he shouted for someone to help. But no one came. Frustrated, he got off his horse to open it himself. Just as he was about to get back on, with one foot in the stirrup, a group of pigs startled his horse. The animal jumped to the side, throwing Michael off balance. He fell against the fence, landing on a sharp wooden post that stabbed him deep in the stomach. He collapsed to the ground, unconscious.

Later that evening, when the peasants returned from the fields, their horses suddenly stopped at the village gate, refusing to go any farther. Looking around, the workers spotted Michael's lifeless body. He lay face down in a pool of blood, exactly where he had fallen.

Only Peter Mikhayeff had the courage to get off his horse and approach him. The others, too afraid to come near, rode around the village and entered through backyards. Peter gently closed Michael's eyes, then placed his body in a wagon and brought it back home.

When the nobleman heard about Michael's death and the cruel way he had treated the peasants, he decided to free them. Instead of forcing them to work for him, he allowed them to rent the land for a small fee and farm it on their own terms.

From that moment on, the peasants understood that true power does not come from cruelty, but from kindness.

Thank You for Reading

Dear Reader,

We hope this timeless classic has sparked your imagination and enriched your literary journey. Now that you've turned the final page, we want to share a vision for the future of reading—one where every classic you've ever wanted to explore is at your fingertips, in a format that best suits your life.

We'd like to invite you to gain immediate, unlimited digital & audiobook access to hundreds of the most treasured literary classics ever written—along with the option to secure deluxe paperback, hardcover & box set editions at printing cost. Together, we can spark a new global literary renaissance alongside our small, independent publishing house called "The Library of Alexandria."

Thousands of years ago, the Library of Alexandria stood as a beacon of knowledge—until it was lost to history. We aim to reignite that spirit of preservation and discovery right now, in the modern age—only this time, it's accessible to all, in every language and every format.

Picture a world where every timeless classic, novel, poem, or philosophical treatise is not only available to read but also updated for today's readers—modernized, translated into any language or dialect, and ready to enjoy in any format you choose, whether that is in an eBook, audiobook, paperback, or deluxe hardcover & box set version a printing cost.

By joining our movement to rebuild the modern Library of Alexandria, you become part of an unprecedented mission to offer:

- **Unlimited Audiobook & eBook Access to the Greatest Classics of All Time**

  Instantly explore thousands of legendary works, from Plato and Shakespeare to Jane Austen and Leo Tolstoy. All are instantly ready to read or listen to, giving you a complete literary universe at your fingertips.

- **Paperback & Deluxe Editions at Printing Costs:**

  Purchase any title in a paperback, deluxe hardbound, or deluxe boxset edition at printing costs, shipped right to your doorstep. Curate your personal library of Alexandria with editions worthy of display— crafted to last, designed to captivate, and delivered straight to your door.

- **Modern translations for Contemporary Readers in all languages and dialects**

  Discover a vast selection of classics reimagined in clear, current language—no more struggling with outdated phrases or obscure references. Next to the original versions, we aim to offer translations in as many languages and dialects as possible.

  As we continue our translation efforts and add new languages, readers everywhere can connect with these works as if they were written today. By bridging linguistic divides, you're contributing to ensuring that these timeless stories become more meaningful, accessible, and inspiring for people across the globe.

- **Your Personal Library of Alexandria:**

  Over the months and years, you'll curate a unique physical archive of classics—each volume a testament to your taste, curiosity, and love of knowledge. It's not just about owning books—it's about curating a cultural legacy you'll cherish and pass down for generations to come.

- **Join a Global Literary Renaissance:**

  Your support fuels an ongoing mission: allowing us to reinvest in offering deluxe print editions (including special boxsets) at their true cost, broaden the range of available formats and translations, and extend the reach of these works to new audiences worldwide. By joining today, you're not just preserving a legacy of masterpieces; you set in motion a powerful wave of literary accessibility.

We are more than a publisher—we're a movement, and we can't do it alone. Your support lets us scale our mission, preserving and reimagining history's greatest works for tomorrow's readers.

Become a Torchbearer of knowledge.

Thank you for picking up this book and allowing us into your literary journey. As you turn the pages, know that you're part of something larger: a global effort to keep these stories alive, share their wisdom across borders and generations, and spark a true cultural revival for the modern era.

If this resonates with you—please consider taking the next step by visiting:

www.libraryofalexandria.com

With gratitude and a shared love of knowledge,

The Modern Library of Alexandria Team

Visit:

www.libraryofalexandria.com

Or scan the code below: